MERAKI: Poetry of the soul

Rumi Sharma

BookLeaf Publishing

India | USA | UK

Presentation by *BookLeaf Publishing*

Web: www.bookleafpub.com

E-mail: info@bookleafpub.com

ISBN: 9789363311428

First edition 2024

ROUTINE

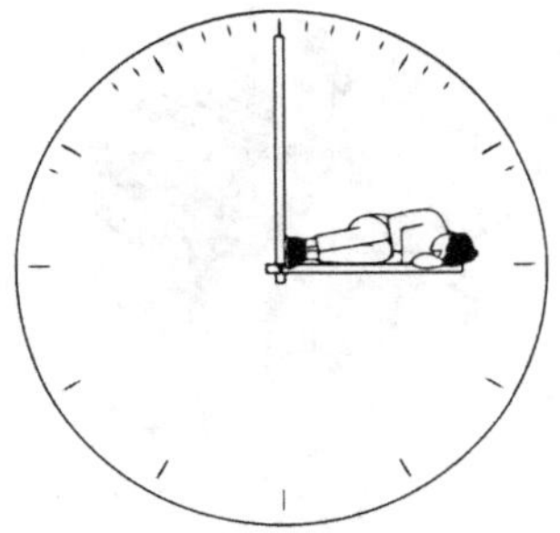

Early rise the feathered friends,
With the paper boy singing the aubade.
Lapsang Souchong from the tea cup
In company with the bulletin and better-half
Starts the day of Average Joe.

Shower, breakfast and the running bus,
Regimed Joe Blow nine to five.
Files, papers, meetings or so...
Engrossed his life for the first half.

Returning home, lie on the sofa
Tranquilling himself the busy-bee.
Watching the TV or browse his smarty
Falls asleep with a sigh.
And redoes till he dies.

****

REALITY

Get up,
Wear the mask,
Get a fixed smile,
Tune the voice with diplomacy.

Back home,
Open the mask,
Ask God for forgiveness;
And continue with the routine...

It's reality.

****

SONG OF A CONCRETED BIRD

Why do I hate those mountains and trees?
Why do I hate the waves of the sea?
Why do I hate the giggling of the river waters?
Why do I hate the wind that passes by me?
Concreted warmth embraces me;
It seems I am somebody else.
I hear one voice in silence, calling my name.
I asked, "Who are you?"
The voice became dumb.
I asked again, "Where are you?"
A voice from miles whispers in my ears,
"Look into your heart, there I am."
I peeped through the door of the heart;
There lay a soul akin to myself.

I asked, "Who are you?"
The soul modestly said, "I am the lost part of
you, in this concreted land."
But I refused to recognise her.
Because I am in love with this concreted soul.

****

RIGHT IN WRONG

Walking through the wrong path
Helps discover the right path
To an unknown goal.

Solving a problem in the wrong way
Is itself a new solution
To another problem in the right way.

Seeking love from someone wrong
Helps recognise the true love of someone right.

Discovering the worth of life in the wrong way
Helps discover death in the right way.

Hence, every right deed has
A wrong beginning in the right way.

****

A JOURNEY THROUGH DREAM

I walked through the path of darkness,
Reached an ambience of solace
Where solitude embraced the princess of light.
Marshalled towards a river of hope and fantasy,
Dream was sailing in that river with its entire
legacy.
I asked the Princess of Light...
Which place is this?
She answered, "It is your lonely heart,
That travels so far to find its company in the
midst of solidity."
I asked the Princess of Light again...
Is there any solution to this aloofness?
She answered with the same modesty...
Time waited for you to medicate it.
And heal it, from the heart of the aloofness.

****

POETRY OF LIFE

Death be the poetry of life!
Echoing the dark shades of pain,
Carried by the pest upon his arms in stain.
Man cried in fear with anxiety and stress;
Blind to see the fine line between pleasure and
pain
And then be at the best.
He ran after money, status and fame,
But ended up in a six-feet land to be one
defamed.

****

SMOKEY LIFE

Life be cheroots or cubas,
One end triggers the birth
Born out of smoke;
And other be the death
On the lips of man's face.

Between is the vain journey of life
Running after a big zero.

****

THE BLUE SEA

The puffy sea
Behold shades of blue,
Enrolling the beauty of the sky.
But the aglitter waves at night
Concedes the pall of silence,
Carried in the heart of a sailor.
Amidst the sea, the sailor cries out for someone
at the distant shore;
He waves his hand and cries out for help,
For he, a muffled male voice in the past years,
A replicate heart of the sailor in the distant sea.

****

JOURNEY OF LIFE

The bus of infancy,
Waits for me outside my mother's womb;
The nurse said, "Hurry up, we are late!"
The time had already started at zero.
I jumped into the bus,
And had my first seat on my mother's lap.
A mischievous road I passed by,
Through tears, smiles, and laughs,
Learnt to crawl, stand, walk, jump and run.
The bus dropped me in the stoppage of
childhood at five,
There stood I with a bag on my back and a flask
hung around my neck;
Wearing a dress just like the others,
Met new people of my height.
This bus took me a long way,
Dropping me in the stoppage of teenhood at
twelve.
This path is frightful and full of adventure,
Should hold my seat tightly, advised my mother.

Reached nineteen, the stoppage of adulthood.
Met new faces in different seats of travel routes.
Strangers they were,
Though close to my heart.
Some got down earlier,
And some went along till I reached the last
stoppage of my life.

****

A QUESTION OF MISTAKE

She was just nine or ten
When you first touched her breast
Choking her childhood
With both your dirty hands.

She was just thirteen or fourteen
When you hit her
Unable to accept a rebellious she.

She was just sixteen or seventeen
When you issued her
A character certificate,
Calling her a characterless slut.

She was just twenty-one
When you sent her
To an unknown house
Killing all her dreams
With your sharp stiff weapon
Called patriarchy.

She was just twenty-two
When she hung herself silently
To release all the pain.

So the question now is
Whose mistake was it?
Yours or hers?

****

THE CARETAKER

He made a coffee for her while she was busy
Preparing papers for her next day colloquy.
He oiled her hair after she returned from the office
Tired and exhausted.
He dropped the children Mamlu and Paplu at school;
Picked them up again after two.
She called him asking, "Did they reach home safely?"
Replied he: "They just had lunch and fell asleep."
There she sighed over the phone.
And said he silently: "Don't worry! Have faith in your lifetime caretaker."

****

ROSE IS RED, SO IS THE BLOOD

His arms around her shoulder
When she is off-mood,
His presence in the dark
When she is all alone,
His smile like a sunbeam
When she is weeping in the dark.
His hands in hers
When she is shivering in fear;
But everything became her past
When he rested his head on her lap,
After fighting his last battle together;
There ends the tale of a lovely wife,
Sitting beside the dead body of her lover.

****

THE DARKER SHADES

The dusky lights
Unveil her cocoon
Deep down the red blood
Entails her body shape.
Enthralled me by her fragrance
Spreads like wildfire,
Rushes through my veins
Inebriates my thoughts of lust.
The child anew the thoughts
Pulls it out of the cocoon,
The darker shades get dazzling
As never before.

****

UGLY but BEAUTIFUL

I am dark,
I am ugly,
Yet I am beautiful.

They say that God was cruel to me,
At the time of my birth,
He forgot to paint me white.

I am dark,
I am ugly,
Yet I am beautiful.

They say, there was space vacant,
To be filled on the earth,
He sent me to the earth without any make-up.

I am dark,
I am ugly,
Yet I am beautiful.

I sometimes wonder,
Is it really so?
Lowering my inner confidence;
I then console myself by saying,
Though my outer appearance may not be nice,
Yet I am beautiful,
I am beautiful from my heart.

God sent me here with a purpose,
Nothing matters whether am fair or dark,
I am beautiful, beautiful from my heart.

I am dark,
I am ugly,
Yet I am beautiful.

Embrace them to feel the warmth of your heart.
'Cause, they are the only ones,
With whom we share the best part of our life.

****

THE QUESTION

Waiting for someone,
Is not a big deal.
But for whom are you waiting?
Is the question.
Knowing and unknown one,
Isn't a big deal.
But how much do you know about him?
Is the question.
Loving someone deeply
Is not a big deal.
But till when?
Is the question.

****

NOTHING BUT SOMETHING

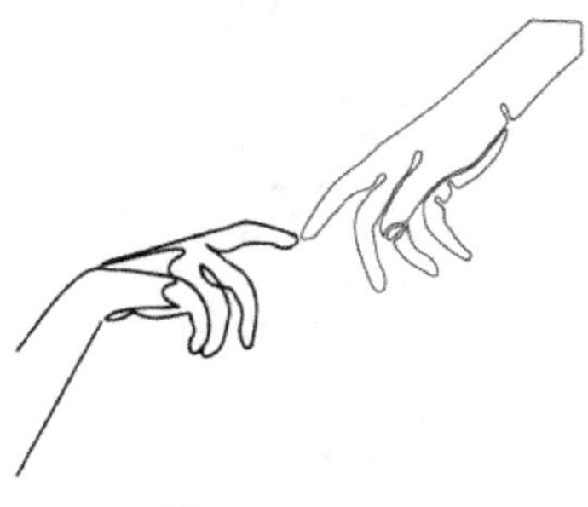

Starred he, starred I
Smiled he, smiled I
Hand-in-hand,
Heart-to-heart.
But suddenly,
Right he went, left I,
Tried we two to meet;
But we were and forever
In two opposite ways.
There was nothing but something.
There ends a story with no beginning.

****

SONG OF THE PAST

A song from the past,
Came floating from the distant land.
Instantly the bird felt a deep fear of solitude,
It searched for a latibule around.
The sense of drapetomania passed through its
veins.
The day was brumous,
Its heart switches the string of the melancholy
tune.
Tried he to abscond from there.
Cause, the bird was in the state of anagapesis.

****

SYMPHONY OF LOVE

Those tiny feet kicking inside the mother's
womb,
Those little ones in the nest fed by their loving
mother,
Those warm hands of the lovers walking beside,
Those morning prayers of the mother seeking
blessing for her dear ones,
Those wakeful hours of darkness of the
newly-weds,
Those evening talks over a cup of coffee of the
old pair,
Those late-night talks and giggles of the
roommates,
Those hugs and kisses of the father on his
daughter's forehead.
All carry the same tune of cheerfulness.
The symphony of love.

****

SONG OF LOVE

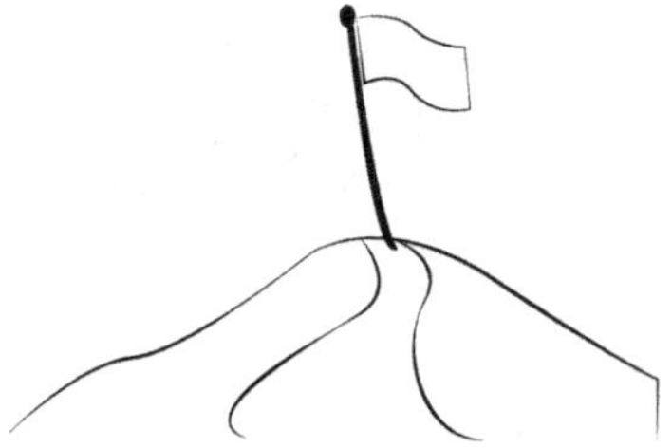

Let love not be the language of the poet,
Time be the currency of life.
The beggars in the sukleswar ghat,
Singing the melancholy tunes of the childhood
homes.

Love not be the language of the lovers,
The advent of the fagun
The unkempt dyed hair,
The criss-cross lines over the forehead,
Growing a little darker;
Singing the song of those desired green.

Love actually be the song of the soldiers, living
on the border,
Fighting in the wars,
And even ready to be wrapped in tricolor.
Whose heroic tales of love
Would be enshrined in gold forever.

****

SOULFUL HARMONY

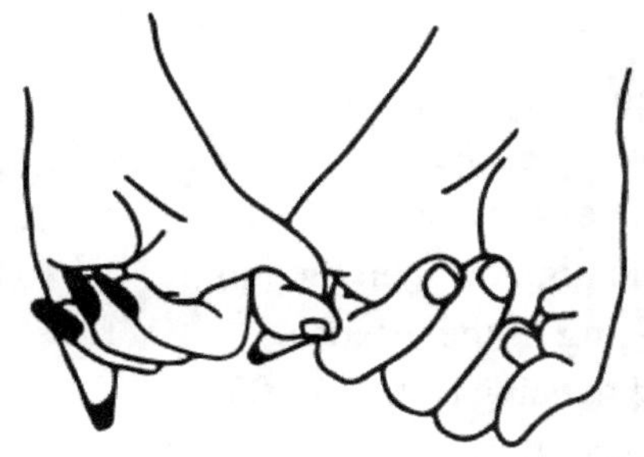

Two hearts, now one,
Bound by love's sweet thread,
Embark on a journey
Where dreams are wed.
In the dance of life,
Their steps entwine,
A melody of love, pure and divine.
Hand in hand,
Through storm and sun,
Their love story has just begun.
A vow to cherish,
To hold,
To keep,
Love embraces, forever deep.

****

SILENCE

The night seems darker,
The hooting of the owl,
From the distant land,
Came floating through the jungle.
The singing of the cicadas
And the dancing of the fireflies
All disappeared.
A pall of silence
Surrounds the ambience.
The sunbeams break through the dawn.

****

THE HIGHWAY

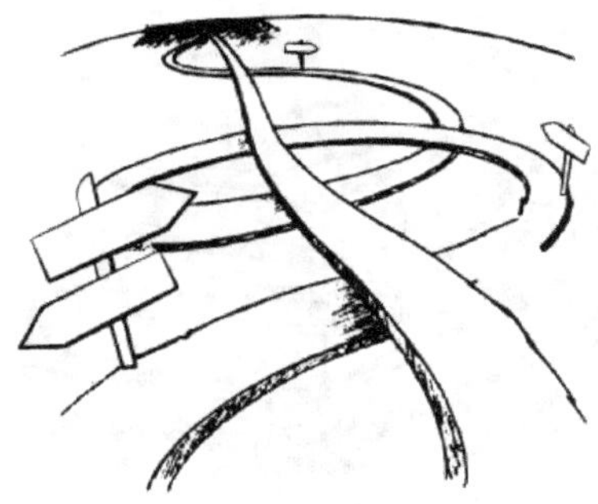

The highway is a river,
A ribbon unfurled.
On the endless highway,
Beneath a canopy of stars,
I find solace in the journey,
No matter how far.
Whispers of the wind,
The hum of tires on the road,
The highway sings a song of journey,
Yet,
Untold.

****

SACRED PAGES

In pages bound,

Our spirits find,
A solace true,
A peaceful mind.

In silent whispers,
They unfold,
Stories rich and
tales of old.

Books are friends
that never part,
Whispering wisdom
to the heart.

Companions still
in the darkest night,
Books bring warmth,
a guiding light.

****

UNBIDDEN INTRUDER

Unbidden, you make your home here,
A trespasser in the night
A spectre of fear.

In the quiet of this forsaken place,
Your presence lingers,
A cold embrace.

You are the unwelcome guest,
Unwavering and bold,
In this house of memories,
Where stories unfold.

****

EMBRACING DAWN

A broken heart finds strength to mend,
From ashes rise, old wounds transcend,
Through pain, through tears, a soul reborn,
Embracing dawn, a brand new morn.

****

RIVERS OF RESILIENCE

34

Like rivers carve the ancient stone,
We too reshape, through time, alone.
In every scar, a story spun,
Of battles fought, and battles won.

****

DAYLIGHT DREAMS

Unveil the curtain,
Open the window,
Let the beam of sunlight come in.
The noise outside disturbs
The slumber of the little Tim.
He's still in the lap of trance,
Dreaming of something unusual.
Cause life without dreams
Is a bird without wings
That cannot fly.

****

MEMORIES OF SCHOOL DAYS

Crayon constellations on classroom skies,
Where dreams took flight
In innocent guise.

Pencil sketches on desks,
Worn with time,
Where imagination soared,
In every rhyme.

Lunchbox stories, shared under the sun,
Where memories flourished
In breaks begun.

Library whispers,
Pages turned with care,
Where minds unfurled
In stories rare.

History whispers,
Echoes of the past,
Where lessons of life,
Forever last.

****

A FRAGRANCE

Whispers of old books,
Ink and dust,
A fragrance that carries,
Memories of wanderlust.
Apple pie, the scent of a childhood home,
Where laughter echoed and dreams roamed,
Vintage cologne,
A grandfather's embrace,
Time travelling through,
Fragrance's grace.
A whiff of cinnamon and apple pie,
A journey back to days gone by.

****

DEVOTION IN FUR

With fur like twilight's gentle hue,
Sam, a guardian of dreams
Loyal and true.
Through fields of laughter,
Sam runs free,
A symphony of boundless joy
His spirit key.
Sam's pawprints on my heart,
A dance of joy and grace,
In every wag,
A tale of friendship,
A cherished embrace.

****

TO MY DAUGHTER AT HER NINETEEN

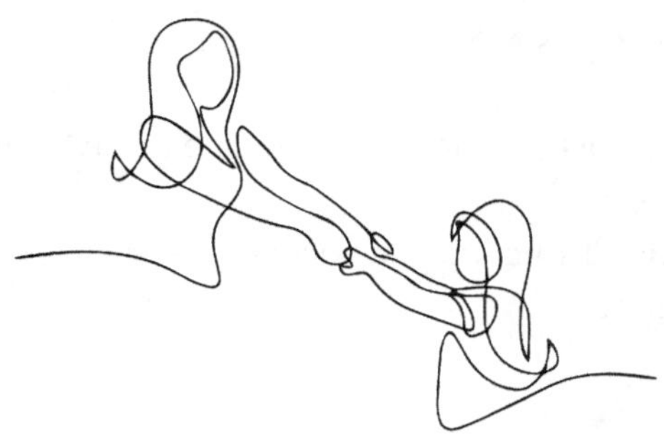

She is the melody in life's symphony,

A sweet song
That lingers in the soul.

In her eyes, I see dreams' waves from starlight,
A future bright

And a future full of endless possibilities.
At nineteen, she stands on the edge of dreams,
A heart full of courage and eyes that gleam.

Her youth is a canvas
She paints with colours
Bold and hues that faint.
Embrace each dawn as a new chance,

And trust that your journey is shaped by both
courage and grace.

Tomorrow shall I be there or not

Remember, my dear, the stars are always yours
to chase,
But don't forget to anchor your heart in
kindness.

****

SONG OF BOHAG

Bohag embraces the world renews,
Blossoms of spring in vibrant hues.
Bohag dances in the fields,

A symphony of green,
With songs of joy.

When Bordoisila sings,
The sky unravels,
Revealing the wild heart of the storm.

In the heart of Assam,
Bihu's flames ignite,
a celebration of harvest, life and light.
Rhythms of the dhol reverberate,

Bihu's spirit in every beat,
A joyful state.

Bohag's breeze whispers tales of old.

Of love,
Of life,
In colours bold.

****

FEARLESS LACHIT
(The Legend of Assam)

In battle's fierce,
Where courage reigns supreme,

Lachit's spirit,
A river unbridled, in every stream,
Amidst the Brahmaputra's embrace,
Where legends rise,
Lachit's valour echoes in the Saraighat War,
Beneath Assam's skies.
Beheaded his own uncle,
For the sake of the motherland,
Everyone was shocked along with the Mughals,

Looking at his truckle.
In every stride,
In every fearless stand,
Bir Lachit's legacy
Engraved on Assam's land.

****

A SOUL'S ILLUMINATION

Beneath neon lights,
Her shadow lingers.
A life mapped by stranger's hands,
Each touch a story,
Each gaze a question.
Her heart a fortress on shifting sands.
Nights blur into a haze of whispers,

Promises lost in smoky rooms
Dreams stitched in silk and tattered lace,
Seeking dawn through the veil of gloom.
Her smile, a mask, a fractured mirror,
Reflecting hopes that never cease,
In the quiet hours, she dreams of freedom,
A silent prayer for a moment's peace.

****

WHEN AUTUMN CAME

Amber leaves dance in the crisp twilight,
Whispering secrets of the harvest moon.
The scent of wood smoke mingles with the chill,
A symphony of endings and beginnings.
In the mosaic of autumn's colours
We see the tapestry of our lives,
Each hue reflects a season of joy, sorrow and
growth.

Lines etched on his face,
Each one a map of
Places, times, and grace.
In the autumn of his days,
He finds new songs in old ways.

****

IN HIS WINTER DAYS

Winter's twilight mirrors the dusk of life,
Where old age scatters wisdom
Like frost upon the earth.
With silver strands and a steady hand,
He holds the past so dear,
A keeper of the stories,
Of all he loved and feared.
His eyes,
Though dim,
Still shine with the fire of bygone days,
Reflecting a life well lived,
In a thousand varied ways.

****

BABY ON HIS STROLLER

A tiny voyager in a world so vast,
Wheels hum softly as the moments pass.
Cradled by the gentle morning breeze,
A baby's laughter mingles with the trees.

In a stroller,
Dreams of future days,
As sunlight weaves through a leafy maze.

Eyes wide with wonder at the sky's expanse,
The stroller glides in a dreamlike dance.

****

CALENDAR

Days turn like pages in the calendar grasp,
Marking time in the lines of a weathered face.

Each month a chapter,
Each year a story told,
The calendar maps the journey of a soul.

With every flip of the calendar,
The man grows older,
Yet his spirit remains timeless,
Forever bolder.

****

A WINTER MORNING

The morning frost draws patterns on the glass,
As the steam from coffee cups ascends and
twirls.
We sit together,
Wrapped in wool and dreams,
The quiet hum of water fills the air.
Your hand in mine,
We trace the past in words.
Each sip a moment savoured,
Soft and warm.
We speak of future days,
Of plans and of hopes,
For in this shared embrace,
We are the spring.

****

THE CAT AND THE FISH

In the quiet shadows of the sunlit room,
The cat with amber eyes and silent tread
Approached the glass where water held its
realm.
Within, a fish of silver scales did glide,
A dancer in its liquid world of blue.
The cat, with patience born of ancient hunts,
Watched every flicker, every darting fin,
Yet paused,
Entranced by beauty unforeseen.
Two lives, divided by a fragile wall,
One bound to land,
The other free to swim;
Both dreaming of a place where worlds could
merge,
Where paws and fins might touch,

If just in dreams.

****

THE HOUSEFLY

The housefly buzzes aimless,
A wanderer in the air,
Man's purpose often fleeting,
Yet burdened by despair.
Both drawn to fleeting moments,
Where light and shadows meet,
In the grand, unwritten saga,
Their paths are incomplete.
The fly finds no tomorrow,
Its world a tiny sphere,
Man's dreams stretch toward forever,
Yet he too disappears.
Both navigate existence,
Each in their own way,
The housefly and the mortal,
In life's ephemeral play.

****

DANCE IN THE RAIN

In the rhythm of raindrops,
We found our dance,
Whispers of rain,
A melody for our feet to trace.
Splashing through puddles,
Our laughter paints the sky,
With each step, rain kissed earth,
Breathes anew sigh.
In the downpour's embrace
We spin tales of love and grace,
Rain's gentle cadence, a lullaby
For our souls to chase.

Dancing barefoot, we become
The rhythm of the storm,
Rain-soaked whispers,
A serenade in nature's form.

****

MANGO PRICKLES

Amidst the mango's golden hue, I find,
A dance of prickles,
Secrets intertwined.

Each thorn, a tale of
Summer's sweet embrace,
A tender sting,
Memories to trace.

In sunlit groves,
Where memories reside,
Mango prickles whisper tales,
Untied.

They guard the fruit of love's eternal play,
And mark the paths where dreams would often
stray.
So let us dance amid the mango's crown,
Where prickles guard the treasures we have
found.

****

CELEBRATING MOTHERHOOD
(Song of a new Mom)

In the quiet hours of dawn,
A mother cradles the world,
Her heartbeats sync with a fragile new song.

Tiny hands grasping,
Eyes wide with wonder,

Each diaper change, a testament to love's tender
labour.
Amidst the soft coos and midnight cries,
A mother finds her strength in the rhythm of
lullabies.

The scent of baby powder lingers in the air,
A reminder that even in chaos,
There's beauty to be found there.
Diapers piled high,
A fortress of care,

Where a mother's love weaves a tale beyond
comparison.

****

GONE ARE THOSE DAYS

The clatter of keys and the shuffle of feet,
A symphony of lives in a harmonious beat.
In corridors lined with memories bright,
Hostel life glows in the heart's twilight.
Simple meals and shared spaces,
Bound by ties,
In endless embraces.
From early dawn to midnight's call,
In the hostel's realm, we've lived it all.
Nights spent under the dimming light,
Stories exchanged till the break of night.
Friendships forged in the furnace of youth,

Hostel life's canvas,
Painted with truth.

****

ROOMMATES

Amid the clutter of our crowded room,
We forge a friendship,
Steadfast as dawn.
Through every laughter and tear,
We carve a path,

A journey marked by unity and grace.
In this small space,
We learn to coexist,

To navigate the world with hearts as one.
Our stories intertwine like ancient roots,
Anchored deep within the soil of home.

In midnight talks,
We find our souls laid bare,
A refuge in the storm of life's demands.
As seasons change,
Our bond remains unchanged,
A testament to friendship's lasting power.

****

LIFE IS A BEAUTIFUL RIDE

Life is a beautiful ride,
Where morning dew glistens on sunlit trails,

And sunsets whisper promises of tomorrow.
Through winding roads and open skies,
Life's journey where each mile blooms with
unexpected wonders.

As we pedal through the seasons,
Life's beauty unfolds in the petals of spring,
And the crisp air of autumn
In the dance of shadows and light,
Life reveals its beauty
In the quiet dawn and the vibrant dusk.

****

MOONLIT MUSINGS

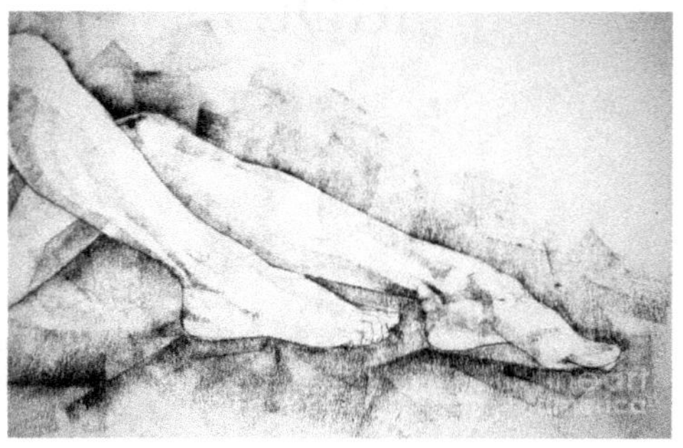

Her legs, slender as moonbeams,
Weave a tapestry of allure
beneath the starlit sky.
With legs that rival the elegance
of a gazelle, she strides through the world,
Leaving trails of wonder.

Her long legs, like ancient columns,
support the temple of her grace,
Each step a testament to beauty.
As she walks, her legs paint silent sonnets,
On the canvas of the earth,
Each line a tribute to their splendour.

Her legs, kissed by the golden light of dawn,
Move with a fluid grace,
That captivates every gaze.

****

LUNAR LULLABY

From my bed,

I watch the moonlight dance through the
window pane,
A serenade of silver whispers easing my weary
brain.
The moon's gentle beams creep through the
glass,

Kissing my slumbering eyes,
As I drift on lunar tides beneath the velvet skies.

Wrapped in sheets of night,
I gaze at the moon's ethereal gleam,
A silent companion to my whispered dreams.

****

IN HER STEPS

She's the queen of drama, with a crown made of
socks,
Turning our house into a stage, and all of us into
props.
She steals my clothes and borrows my shoes,
Yet somehow still blames me when she gets a
bruise.
A walking tornado of laughter and chaos,

She can turn a quiet room into a riotous fiesta.
She's got a heart of gold but a penchant for
pranks,
Leaving me wondering, "What's next from her
bag of tricks?"
With a smile that says "trouble" and a laugh
that's contagious,
My sister's mischief is both endless and ageless.

****

TO HER FATHER

The strength in his gaze, a fortress of care,
A silent guardian, always there.

When she was small, he'd lift her to the sky,
In his eyes, the stars shone, lighting up the night.

Through every stumble, every tear that fell,
In his eyes, she saw a love that words couldn't
tell.

On her wedding day, as she took his arm,
In his eyes, a blend of pride and tender alarm.

****

TO HER MOTHER

In her chubby cheeks, I find my home,
A jolly spirit where my heart can roam.
Short in height, but tall in grace,
Your love, dear mother, time can't erase.
Your fat and happy laughter rings,
A melody of joy life brings.
In your embrace, I feel so free,
Dear mother, you're the world to me.

****

DIGITAL ECHOES

In the glow of screens, we weave our tales,
a digital dance of likes and shares.
Silent whispers in the virtual air,
friendships forged with a single click,
fragile as a pixel's flick.
Our lives, a tapestry of posts and tweets,
where moments are measured by re-tweets.
Echo chambers where voices blend,
a cacophony that never ends.
Beneath the filters and curate smiles,
The search for meaning spans digital miles.
In the vast expanse of online seas,
we lose ourselves in endless feeds.

****